A SOLDIER POET

Published in paperback by SilverWood Books 2010

www.silverwoodbooks.co.uk

ISBN 978-1-906236-29-8

British Library Cataloguing in Publication Data
A CIP catalogue record for this book is available from
The British Library

Set in 11.5pt Bembo by SilverWood Books

Printed in Great Britain by Cpod, Trowbridge

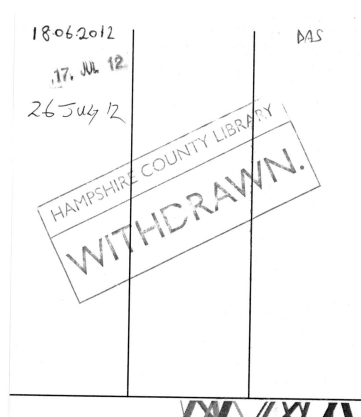
Get **more** out of libraries

Please return or renew this item by the last date shown.

You can renew online at www.hants.gov.uk/library

Or by phoning 0845 603 5631

Hampshire
County Council

A SOLDIER POET

Memoirs of Afghanistan and Iraq

ALEX ROISSETTER

SilverWood

ACKNOWLEDGEMENTS

*A huge thank you to all those that have helped in the
making of this book, especially my mum, family
and Katherine Hook as editors.*

*All those that are in the military fighting for the freedom of
others out in Afghanistan, Iraq, the Balkans and all the other
tours of duty in the past, present and future.
May you return home safely and in good health.*

*Big thank you to the members of forcespoetry.com
(I am a proud moderator of the site) in helping me get my poetry
out there, and giving me the drive to make my work into this
book. Good luck in trying to become a charity for those that are
suffering from PTSD (Post Traumatic Stress Disorder) either
from the act of war or other traumatic events.*

*A big thank you to Tom McGreevy (head moderator of
forcespoetry.com) for letting me be on the front cover of his own
book* I'm A Soldier...Get Me Out Of Here! *I love the
book and all the work he does on the site with Mac Macdonald
(founder of forcespoetry.com).*

*Finally big thanks to B.J. Lewis for giving me permission to
use one of his own awesome poems in my book
and also Garron Hilton for taking some amazing pictures that
go so well and paint a solidarity with my own work.*

Contents

A SOLDIER POET

THE WANDERING

I feel like I'm off the map,
And my compass doesn't know where to point,
My energy is starting to sap,
With an aching in my joint.

My heart tells me to go on,
To my journey's end,
Where I can hear my song,
A place I can stop and mend.

Over the fields of battle I roam,
Taking in the dusty smell,
My mind wanders back to home,
With a story that I can tell.

The Wandering

This was the very first poem that I wrote. I still remember being in my bed whilst I was on my second tour (the first one in Qatar then Afghanistan) trying to get to sleep when the first line popped into my head from absolutely nowhere. It nagged at me for a while until I wrote it down thinking that it would be the end of it. As soon as I did so I could see the next line already forming after it. This is how I now write my poetry in that I do not think or know how any of my poems are going to end when I start writing them or even which meandering course they will take on the way to the finish.

This poem itself is quite straightforward in its content. It's about walking across the desert being weary and tired, as you may have guessed by reading it. On the way seeing the battlegrounds on the land, just wishing that you could be home instead and able to tell someone about it.

Dies Irae

With burning smoke and bullets' spray,
Here comes the wrath of days,
Like a creeping fog in early May,

Here comes the *Dies Irae.*

With rocket's scream and grenade's throw,
Here comes the wrath of days,
So much blood where death will sow,

Here comes the *Dies Irae.*

With mortar blow and bomb's strike,
Here comes the wrath of days,
Wherever you go heads on a pike,

Here comes the *Dies Irae.*

With Child's tears and bellies bloat,
There goes the wrath of days,
Rivers filled with bodies float,

There goes the *Dies Irae.*

With winter chill and cockroach scuttle,
There goes the wrath of days,
And if it's just not obviously subtle,

Here comes the *Dies Irae.*

13th October 2007

Dies Irae

This was one of my early poems that I wrote while I was half way through my tour in Afghanistan. The title is actually said as 'dye es I ray', otherwise it might translate into something unimaginable. Dies Irae, however, translates to "Wrath of Days" and this poem was originally titled "Dies Irae (Wrath of Days)" but I shortened it to just the Latin. I wanted a poem that was almost like a march of war, almost like on the parade ground but with the chaos of battle. Even though war has swept across the land, destroying nearly everything in its path leaving so much destruction it comes back again at the end. There is no end to war; the only thing that changes is the location.

I chose the words Dies Irae because I wanted a different language to mix into my poetry (this comes up again in more of my poems). The words are part of the Requiem Mass, and were also the name of a war machine in a science fiction book that I was reading at the time. When I found out what they meant it fell neatly into place.

Going to Launder

"You're going to war!"
The colonel said,
"To have RPGs shot at your head,
Some might even end up dead."

"Yours is a vital role,
Sat behind a desk,
So don't sell your soul,
I know you will protest."

Doing the laundry,
It's a wondrous thing,
Cleaning the skid marks,
Of the fighting machine.

It will soon be your turn
To be at the front,
'Stead of cutting the lawn,
And to be on the hunt.

But watch what you wish for,
Cos it might be a mistake,
To be on tour;
O what a tombstone you'll make.

13th October 2007

Me in the security box to HQ RC (S). I was there to check ID cards and a small information desk amongst other jobs. Kandahar Airfield, Afghanistan.

Going to Launder

This poem was written near the end of my tour in Afghanistan after I had changed jobs from being embedded with the Pioneers (23 Pioneer Regiment) to being in administration for the HQ (RC-S). This job ranged from booking in the washing of the senior staff to being security to the two compounds, which was extremely boring as you might imagine, especially as during the first four months of the tour I had been providing communications for The Pioneers, escorting VIP's into Kandahar City and other general patrols. So this poem is a bit of a joke and prods a stick at what we had to do.

When I asked a man in a London street what he thought of my poems he read this one and mentioned that it was very similar to Siegfried Sassoon's "The General" which starts with a high ranking officer saying "Good Morning" to private soldiers as they went past to battle. When we were told that we were going to Afghan to fight we thought that we would be getting in the thick of it in Helmand Province. But in the end only a very few actually left Kandahar Airfield (KAF) itself so I was glad that I was picked to be one of the few that did.

17

THE LONELY ROAD

We walk down the lonely road,
In a distant place,
Of a land untold,
Far away from where it's safe.

The heat is unbearable in this town,
With heavy sweat in the eyes,
Their faces always a frown,
Covering up those untold lies.

The people that you have to watch,
With eyes of rage,
And a prayer shouts,
With a push we turn the page.

With everyone that mourns and weeps,
For the soldiers,
And people on the streets,
Digging them from the boulders.

The killers do not blame,
For they believe,
With hope as a flame,
But only the innocent we grieve.

As a country we want it to cease,
Carry the load,
To lead the world to peace,
As we all walk down the lonely road.

The Lonely Road

"The Lonely Road" is about being on patrol in Afghan and trying to figure out who we are actually fighting in the crowd because, to the westerners' eyes, all the people over there look the same in dress and speech and the enemy intermingles easily with this crowd. Unfortunately finding out who the enemy are can come way too late; as in this poem a bomb was detonated and had covered both soldiers and innocent civilian bystanders alike in debris and boulders. Also at the end of the poem I put that we should not hate the enemy but respect what they are fighting for, as they believe that they are right and just. This was an early poem and was the third poem I actually wrote while I was in Afghan where my poetry started to blossom.

THE OTHER VIEW

You sold your soul to Queen and country,
(It's a shame the food's all lumpy,)
You always say you have no money,
But where we are it's always sunny.

They say that you have no equipment,
And there's always trouble with enlistment,
But as we sit here on our arses,
We see that there are always classes.

The numbers are falling they say,
But they don't join for a game to play,
We heard that war is loud,
And no matter what, they make us proud.

The Other View

This is another early poem that I wrote in Afghanistan. This poem is a bit stern about the government... about how they are not listening to the needs of the Armed Services, and the need for more funds, equipment and to try and bring in more recruits; even though they always say that they are fully behind the Forces in what they are doing in Afghanistan and Iraq, clearly they are not and the civilian population is becoming more aware of this.

On another foot patrol. We saw this little donkey tied up at the side of the street. Basra, Iraq.

Ponder It All

I sit here to think and ponder,
Of all the minutes gone by,
Sometimes of things that might lie yonder,
It all just might be a lie.

There are things that great men think,
Who gaze down the scope to the world beneath,
But others like to miss and make a stink,
To groan aloud and bare their teeth.

All things do not come easy,
For all those in times like these,
But people are just too sleazy,
And it's not much of a tease.

If you always try and fail,
Like so many have done before,
Don't just run away with tail,
Because fate is knocking on your door.

Ponder It All

I wrote this poem outside the admin office in which I worked for two months near the end of my Afghan tour (April–November 2007), while I was waiting for one of my friends to finish work so we could get a hot chocolate and relax a bit after a hard day's work. I was sitting down in the smoking area and I was actually thinking about my choices that I had made that brought me to that spot in which I now found myself. I wondered if it was the best I could have done, and if I had stayed at school for longer then would I be somewhere else entirely doing a different job.

Then I realised that there are a lot of people who argue about such things and analyse them but I am not normally such a person; I have my own philosophy of duty (though many also may have a similar one) and that's to grab anything that comes your way and not to run away from it because it may be the best thing that ever happened to you or a great learning experience in the process. I certainly do not have many regrets about joining the Army.

FIGHT FOR CHRISTMAS

It's been a year to the day,
But I feel so alone and far away,
From snow and stockings on a mantle,
My boots filled with sand to my ankle.

They say it's THAT time on the news,
But we're still wearing helmets on the loos,
The decorations may be a'hangin',
But there's still fighting up in Sangin.

Outside you hear a sleigh bell,
But for us there is still only hell,
On your sofa reading a mag,
Not thinking of us while we're on stag.

A kid sucking a frosty lolly;
For us there's a medic, fixing Tommy,
How many times have we come near it?
While we fight for your Christmas spirit.

While you're on your traditional walk,
Stop, think of us, or maybe just talk,
Your Christmas pudding might be lovely,
But we are dying for Queen and country.

Fight for Christmas

This has been said to be a very strong poem in that it has two different views, one of the everyday civilian and the other of a soldier in Afghanistan. I was on leave from tour from Afghan and I was also changing regiments from 2 Signal Regiment (York) to 7 Armoured Brigade (Hohne, Germany) so I was blessed with extra time off. I was with my ex-girlfriend Sarah at the time and I had come over to visit her at work. While I sat down drinking a beer as she worked, I picked up a pen and a scrap piece of paper that came out of the till. I think she was quite shocked at how fast I can actually write a complete poem and how single-minded I can become when I actually get down to it.

I have been told that this piece is one of most people's favourites and always comes up when they tell someone else about my work. The lines *"A kid sucking a frosty lolly, for us there's a medic, fixing Tommy"* is particularly strong because it sets a picture that shows the complete opposites of each person. The context that I used Tommy was not only as a name but also as the old Tommy in which British soldiers were once called eighty years ago in the Great Wars.

Apaches draped in snow whilst on an exercise in Bavaria building up to the Iraq tour. Germany.

MISTAKE IN THE DARK

Here's me sitting at the bar,
Sipping my frosty beer,
Thinking of life and what happened so far,
And how it always brings a tear.

How different I was back then,
Working in the sun so hot,
Beside these sweaty sunburnt men,
Like chilli and lime in a pot.

Driving through the streets so dusty,
The locals, so dark and suspect,
Tension so buttery and musty,
All it takes is the glimpse of a musket.

Rounds shoot off, BANG!
Follow that ghostly glimmer,
Our guns from top-cover sang,
Everyone dives for cover and gives a shiver.

No shot came back,
We wonder what we hit,
Was it the enemy about to attack?
All we can do is ready the medic.

As we shone light into the shadowy darkness,
Came a sight that made us sick,
The kid had a look so very youngish,
If only the shooter had really missed.

Looking back now with pint in hand,
I can still see the kid's eyes of dead fear,
And his soul drifting to another land,
It wells my eyes with a misty tear.

19th December 2007

Mistake in The Dark

I can hardly remember writing this poem but I can imagine that it was around the similar time as I wrote "Fight For Christmas". It was hidden on my computer in the dark recesses of the software until I had a proper look around and rediscovered it.

As you can read in the poem it describes an incident that had happened on a patrol and the person that was looking back at the incident is being haunted by it even when he is back home.

This poem is not about me but the people that may be suffering from PTSD (Post Traumatic Stress Disorder). But I did not realise that it did until I uncovered it and re-read it then thought about what it could be about.

On a Lynx flight deploying to swap a non-functional Tacsat radio on a build-up exercise. Bavaria, Germany.

LADS AT JOURNEY'S END

Home is the ideal we hold,
Even as the last is sold,
In the bright depths of our hearts,
With friends we hide our dark masks.

We clutch it like a life line,
Maybe this dream is not just mine,
With guys that I hardly know,
That words can't bring us low.

Home is what we fight for,
Hoping that we will see it more,
The kingdom safe we shed our blood,
To drown them in a river's flood.

When the enemy is gone,
The people will sing our song,
A wreath of poppies they will send,
For the lads at journey's end.

Lads at Journey's End

I wrote this poem when I was having lunch one time in Al Qurnah (Iraq) with the platoon I was attached with. It got changed in a few places quite often and might do in the future as poems do. When one of the lads up there read it he agreed whole heartedly with the lines "With guys that I hardly know, That words can't bring us low" especially in my case as I had only just been embedded with them for a few weeks at that time.

The poem itself is about how we will always fight till the end; even drown them with our blood until we get to "journey's end" which is of course the afterlife. But it also mentions how we remember the ones that went before us in the fight and how a wreath of poppies is laid down on Remembrance Day for them when there is finally peace for them and us in the future.

FORGOTTEN HONOUR

The honour has left the spire,
Of the nation that was proud to be,
The island of the golden empire,
From shore to wondrous sea.

There is none left who knows it,
No-one who has the sweet taste,
For it has fallen into the pit,
And has cracked and crumbled into waste.

The glue of the world cannot fix,
And tape cannot bind,
Together with history it does mix,
Making it impossible to find.

But they say there's always hope,
Cos it's there for everyone to read,
The old empire will cope,
But from its soldiers it will bleed.

With each drop of blood that's sown,
Will fill the pit burning hot,
And in the end that's all alone,
The reborn honour floats on top.

21st June 2008

Forgotten Honour

"Forgotten Honour" is also a very strong poem. It is about how Britain has lost the sense of honour we once had back in the olden days. It used to be an honour just to be British and fight for a country that you believe in. I cannot pinpoint the time in which this happened but it started to happen after WW2 and even more after the Falklands if we put a military timetable on it. In the poem I describe Britain as "the island of the golden empire"; this is because when we did have an empire we were (and of course still are) only a small country and we expanded so much around the globe. Kick starting other civilisations into being, as it were, and on the way losing our honour as we gave back more and more of our "conquered" areas. But in the end after losing so much our Armed Forces are still fighting for a cause in the defence of Britain and her shores, even if it is in the boundaries of other countries, and in doing so unwittingly keeping the honour that everyone in the British Isles used to have.

If the feeling of honour is to be returned to "the spire" (I imagined it to be a lighthouse that guides our nation to where it needs to go) then the Armed Forces is where it will come from in the sacrifices and memories that the soldiers make with their lives.

THE GLANCE OF DEATH

There's a smell to war we learn to know,
It's in places we sometimes go,
It's in the heathers; it's in the streams,
For you it really must seem obscene.

The blood dyed red on our shaking hands,
As thick as the golden burning sands,
Our conscience fights the aching pain,
And turns into The Mark of Cain.

Never-ending reoccurring nightmare,
After the glance of death we remember the stare,
Until finally it comes back to see,
And takes us away and then we are free.

19th June 2008

The Glance of Death

This is one of the first of my hidden poems that I found in the recesses of my laptop while I was rifling through the software. I was quite surprised that I could hardly remember writing it. When I entered the poem into this book I changed the title from "The Glimpse of Death" to "The Glance of Death" as it sounded a lot more rounded and it fits with the subject matter of the poem. This change of title also meant that I had to change a few lines of the poem.

The reference to "The Mark of Cain" was originally something else and that was changed as well to make the poem a little darker than it was. Of course "The Mark of Cain" was the stigma that was put on Cain in the Bible. It was also the name of a program that featured the torture of Iraqi prisoners that were under the care of British soldiers in the early stages of the second war with Iraq. This is a job that I also did for a few months in Iraq years after the initial incident and so there were a lot more restrictions and monitors in place to make sure it didn't happen again.

SHINE FOR THE LOST

Where is the road that was lit so bright?
That our sodden feet followed like rails,
How many are lost to the bitter fight,
From the bullets driven like jagged nails?

The shoulders of the nation are falling short,
Of the plateau of the brave volunteers,
That do not ask for any support,
But to remember those that deserve our tears.

What have they lost when they sign?
Their lives not their own is the price,
And hope one day that life will shine,
Even though it's rolled with loaded dice.

So shine the torch where these lost men tread,
On the winding road that returns to the kingdom,
And honour the memories of the fallen dead,
That lost the roll in the name of freedom.

26th June 2008

On the roof of Cimic House in Al Qurnah, the MiTT (Military Transition Team) OC with one of his Cpls looking over the city at sunset. Iraq.

Shine for the Lost

This poem is about how I felt that the British public had forgotten or ignored the Armed Forces while they were fighting out on tour. This is a subject quite close to my heart, as one might fathom from a few more of my poems on this subject. I wrote this poem quite early in my tour in Iraq when I was attached to The Poachers (4plt, B Company, 2nd Battalion, The Royal Anglian Regiment) up in Al Qurnah supplying communications for them.

MEMORIES WITH PRIDE

How many days have you sat and prayed,
While the child inside you runs and plays?
Clenched knuckles white with fear,
And fading memories you held so dear.

Thoughts match a broken body of scars,
That nearly fell to the place of stars,
Old and weary from the past,
Afraid to think that you're the last.

The bonds of the fighting force,
Are forever strong even when coarse,
The brotherhood line is like an evergreen flower,
Even as you sit there hour by hour.

The pictures you stare at on the mantle with pride,
Are faded from thumb prints on the side,
After a while you always smile,
Even after walking the murder mile.

10th July 2008

Memories with Pride

I wrote this poem while I was on the COB (Coalition Operational Base) in Iraq near Basra. I was sat having a strawberry milkshake. Just before I had been reading a poetry book from Siegfried Sassoon who was a poet from WW1 and it got me thinking. What would it feel like to have fought in that conflict and survived to this day, maybe being the only one left. The character had obviously been wounded and nearly died from these wounds. He still thinks back to the time of the war with the people that he fought alongside. The "brotherhood line" is mentioned because in war a bond of brotherhood is formed with the man next to you that can't be broken even after such a long time. Right at the end I have also mentioned something about "the murder mile", this is the area we commonly call "no man's land". During the first Great War it was common for the soldiers to be ordered to go over the top and walk towards the enemy because it was the last thing they would be expecting even though they were prepared for so much more. Will I be like this when I am old looking back on my life and what I have done? Who knows?

LITTLE MOZZIE

Little mosquito, how much you bug me so,
The way you buzz in my ear refusing to go,
Are you wise in knowledge that I am not?
As you buzz around the candle pot.

You annoy me to the core of my being,
It's my blood that you're always seeing,
Your wings flap in your general location,
And just one bite, DAMN THAT SENSATION!

It's amazing how many ways men can kill,
But one little bite can make them ill,
Just one moment is all it takes,
A bite to the grave, that's what it makes.

You see now why I hate you so,
Why your buzzing brings my hand so low,
To try and hit you on the head,
That's another one of the bastards dead.

11th July 2008

Little Mozzie

This seems a much-liked poem with nearly everyone that reads it. I think that's because it flows well and that it's about how such a small creature can be very annoying and seems to know when to strike and eludes being squished a lot of the time. I was up in Al Qurnah lying down outside on my cot bed that was encapsulated in a mosquito net. Normally when I have a bit of inspiration for a piece I have to write it down before I forget due to my dyslexia; that then started a cycle of not being able to go to sleep until it is finished. But this poem was different in that after I thought of a few lines in my head I rolled over and fell asleep, not remembering it until I went back to bed the next night.

This happened twice and I got quite annoyed for not writing it down before but also for forgetting a few words or even lines here and there, so I had to start the first line from scratch a few times. When we first got to Al Qurnah there were not enough mosquito nets to go around so some of us had to sleep outside in the elements and of course the bloodsucking critters that are so fondly squashed under the palm at the end of this poem were out with a vengeance at the time.

DUTY

"Why did you join?"
I'm always asked,
"Was it the tempt of coin?"
One I've always surpassed.

"Was it for the thrills?
Or maybe failed a few tests?
Was it maybe for the kills?"
All I say is "to be the best".

"Will you ever get out?
And live like a slob?"
She asks with a pout,
"There is always a safer job."

"How lonely it must be,
In a place that's always sunny,"
I say "yes, family is hard to see,
And it's not only for extra money."

"And all the dangers you face?"
If I was another I'd get snooty,
And be on their case,
But I just say "yes, I do my duty."

Duty

"Duty" was an attempt poem, so to speak. I have a few in little cubbyholes waiting for the light of day when I believe that they are close to being finished. I cannot say when they are finished because I am always tweaking my poems here and there, like a painter never being satisfied, I am like this with my work as well. This poem is about a conversation that most soldiers have when they talk to an interested civilian. They always ask, "Why did you join?" and they nearly always ask other questions straight afterward. This was my attempt to answer it but I believe that it is a long way from finished and it might take a long time until it is settled. Another question that soldiers are asked is, "Have you ever killed/shot anyone?" The trouble with this question is that if the soldier has then it might dredge up unpleasant memories which he was trying to forget.

Me and Pte Lungu on the back of an Iraqi Army pickup truck (6 Plt B Coy) in Basra City. You can see the antenna of the radio on my back that I carried around.

41

WE ARE THE ONES...

We are the ones, who are proud,
The silent ones that don't make a sound,
Like ghosts we flicker from the shadows,
The shiver that shoots down your marrows.

We are the ones without burning hate,
The professional ones who are never late,
Either in ice or the desert sun,
This is what we call fun.

We are the ones, who never tire,
Even as we look out across the mire,
Through the endless bogs of dried mud,
We trace the ones with guilty blood.

We are the ones, who tread the path,
And in death's face we do laugh,
In battle we fight till the end,
And to God, the fallen dead we send.

We are the ones you forget,
Whose days and nights are not a test,
You are the ones without a story,
And do not shed blood for peaceful glory.

3rd August 2008

Out on a vehicle patrol in the marshes north of Al Qurnah. We found this boat laying there, the vehicle that we're in is a Mastiff, you can see one in the top right of the picture. Iraq.

We Are The Ones...

The poem "We Are the Ones..." is a piece about the divide between the servicemen of today and civilians, and how we put our lives on the line. This is especially poignant with the infantry that are going out "on the ground" in Afghanistan, Iraq and other operations that happen in the past, present and future. They are the ones that actually do the dirty work against the enemy and they are the ones that can claim this right in what they do. Not many people (even in other corps and services) can put their name on that list of actually going to fight.

Most of the personnel that go on tour are administrative roles rather than going out and actively looking for the enemy. There are attachments that join onto these men to supply vital roles such as communications, medics, linguists, vehicle mechanics, etc. But even then these roles are few and far between.

I believe myself to be very lucky to have been picked to be embedded with a multiple of infantry units when they go out of the safe areas in both Afghanistan and Iraq and I am proud of myself that I have been able to do the job that I was trained to do while I was in operations. Also in the last stanza it's as if these men are talking to the civilians who they have the opportunity to serve, and who will have better lives in doing so.

THE ROYAL CORPS

The Royal Corps is our name,
And sending signals is our game,
Every conflict that you see,
Is a part of our proud history.

In every camp, in every town,
Is our backyard, our own playground,
We send along The Boss's orders,
To transmit across the borders.

If you are interested but have no clue,
We can always enlighten you,
On where to find that radio station,
And maybe antennas and propagation.

No matter what we're always training,
Even if it's always raining,
And if there aren't any comms,
The angels cannot drop any bombs.

We are the first to fly, last to go,
Our proud motto is Certa Cito,
And to the end this poem I will shout,
With a press of pressel and a 'roger out'.

22nd August 2008

The pennant of 207 Signal Squadron flying over the entrance to Allenby Lines, Contingency Operations Base, Iraq. Picture by Garron Hilton

The Royal Corps

I wrote this poem to try and explain what my job entails and what it is like.

There are quite a few times in my life where I have tried to do this and failed miserably and probably more often than not making the person that I am trying to explain it to even less interested in the Royal Corps of Signals that I originally intended. So this is the best way to try and explain something in my career.

Most of my poems try to tell the mostly unwitting civilian of what we go through while we are out on tour. Although this poem is not as popular with the other servicemen who are not in the Signals, I think this is mainly due to the rivalries in the services. But even then they can still identify that it is exactly what we do as signallers. In ending the poem I have written "And to the end this poem I will shout, With a press of pressel and a 'roger out'."

This was an idea that I had that most people who have never

been schooled in talking over a radio properly might not get. This is called voice procedure and it comes with quite a few rules, from an obvious one of no swearing to only being able to transmit for twenty seconds before asking the receiving end if they have that part of the message (if it's a long message). This is mainly to cut down on the enemy being able to find out our locations via our radiation emissions. The "roger out" itself is a pro-word to state that we have received the message and that we are now ending the conversation. Civilians are probably more aware of the "over and out" that Hollywood use. This is completely wrong due to the fact that it is two pro-words in one statement and can cause confusion and will definitely come with consequences of buying a crate of alcoholic beverages for the controlling station, when time and rules allow.

Summer Rest in Winter

Stepping off the plane from the sun,
Teeth chattering away,
The lad in front exclaims a wild pun,
Wishing secretly that we could stay.

From hot desert to freezing Blighty,
Forever in her winter chill,
The difference is not felt lightly,
Warm up! Arms revolving like a mill.

Can't wait to see the lads down the Crown,
Drink till the last bell,
To laugh and wash away the frown,
Trying not to think of the return to hell.

16th September 2008

Summer Rest in Winter
I wrote this poem when I was in the middle of my R and R (Rest and Recuperation − a two week leave gap granted for personnel on tour). I was visiting London to read a few of my poems in the Poetry Café that resides down an alley opposite the Cross Keys pub in Covent Garden. This café is a very small place but it has a very contemplative atmosphere.

Normally during the day there are tutors going through the work of their pupils' poetry or other work and giving advice to anyone who is in need of it. At night it will become a different place as there is normally an event on in the basement. This varies from an open mike night to other poetry themed events. I was sat at one of the tables having a beer when I started to write it.

The poem itself was originally about how on each of the three tours that I have done (Qatar, Afghanistan and Iraq) all of them were over summer which means that every time I came back home the UK (Blighty in the poem's case) was always in winter chill. The way it came out was completely different because I let the poem write itself as usual because I never plan a poem from start to finish. The way it turned out was describing what it was like turning up back in England after being in a desert country no longer than twenty-four hours before, and how cold it can be compared between the two. Also when a soldier gets home they will almost always have a few drinks with their friends and family, and try not to think about going back out to complete the rest of the tour in ten to fourteen days.

His Last Parade

The weight of him on our shoulders,
The faint whiff of gunpowder smoulders,
It's almost as if my lead bearing heart,
Would stop with this solemn task.

We step in, out, in, out, in, out,
These timings are not a shout,
To the tune of the bagpipes playing,
To attention he is marching, laying.

Our arms underneath him for support,
To take him to his last call of port,
No longer will he be a trencher,
As the Padre swings his golden censer.

The memories of him will never fade,
As he is carried to his last parade,
He had fought in line with his brothers,
And today he says goodbye to his lovers.

We raise a glass to his name,
Because he lived without any shame,
Now in peace he lies in restful sleep,
And for him we shall forever weep.

23rd September 2008

R.I.P. Scott Barsby

His Last Parade

This poem is very important to me and is said to be extremely strong with emotion. I wrote this when I was watching detainees that had been picked up in Basra but the story has nothing do with this.

The story itself was about my Afghan tour a year earlier and about an incident that occurred shortly after I moved to my new unit in Germany. Everyone is aware of the servicemen that give up their lives in Afghanistan, not only from Britain but also from the Canadians, Estonians, French, Germans, Americans and all the other NATO countries that have personnel in the country. When there is an unfortunate loss of life then there is a ceremony called a repatriation.

This is the marching of the coffins from the temporary morgue in theatre to the transport aircraft which will fly the body to the country which the service man or woman came from. Due to my height and working in the admin office I was "volunteered" to be one of the coffin bearers in most ceremonies. In the end of the tour I had done this job around twenty-five times. Not only for the British dead but also for the other nations that were on the camp as well, except for the Americans who did their own repatriation ceremonies. You can tell that this affected me in a certain way when you read this poem.

As you can also see that this poem is also dedicated to Signaller Scott Barsby who unfortunately lost his life when a drunk driver collided with him on the Celle to Hohne road in Germany. He was only nineteen and was very much looking forward to his first tour with the army. Again I was picked to be a coffin bearer for his funeral back in Derby which his family and friends would be attending. I nearly refused, mainly because I had literally only just finished my Afghan tour a few months before and it brought back a lot of bad memories for me. But even with this I did what I was asked of me because it was my duty to do so. Scott was a brilliant young man who had the personality of about three normal men combined. When morale had dropped in the Squadron then he would be there to bring it back up again.

A Repatriation ceremony at Kandahar Airfield (KAF). The coffin is that of an Estonian, I am at the back left. Afghanistan.

At the funeral itself we were told not to show any emotion in our drill but I really could not help myself. The Union Flag that was draped over his coffin was folded up and passed to his parents together with his boots, belt and forest cap; this was extremely emotional for me and when we were marched out of the crematorium tears were rolling down my cheeks. I could not bring myself to write about it until that moment in Iraq nearly six months on when I was talking to an American about my experience in Afghanistan. The poem itself is about a soldier that was killed in his duty and being carried to "His Last Parade" to the transport plane and later to the cemetery or crematorium.

NIGHT PATROL

Patrolling during the night,
It's dark as pitch without a light,
Hoping that everything will be fine,
And that no one will cross the line.

The radio that's on my back,
Is starting to weigh like a potato sack,
Making sure that we still have comms,
Occupying my weary mind with dirty songs.

My clothes are soaked with sweat,
Determined eyes and my jaw is set,
We've been going on for hours,
Knowing we're not superman with powers.

Getting close back to camp now,
The fellas can go back to Slough,
We patrol past that last pine,
Then it happens, my foot steps on a mine.

27th September 2008

Night Patrol

*I got the inspiration for "Night Patrol" after I came back off
R and R. I was put on guard for the camp that my troop was in.
This lasted for twenty-four hours and you can be very tired from
lack of sleep at the end. While I was standing on the front gate
reading the standard operating procedures (guidelines of a duty/
tasking in the Army) I noticed a little list of what the guard was
comprised of. Of course Night Patrol was one of them and I felt
a little click in my head of what I now know is an idea of a start
of a poem. I wrote the line down for later reference and started to
write the poem itself as soon as I got off for a break. It's about how
while being on a foot patrol I am nearly always the signaller (as is*

Me and MiTT OC with 6 Platoon B Company, 2nd Battalion , The Royal Anglian Regiment (The Poachers) out on foot patrol with the Iraqi Army in Basra City. Iraq.

my role and job) and that there is a main worry for me whenever I go out on such patrols and that is to mentally switch off and then miss something that can cause injury or a death to one of my comrades or to me and potentially put the mission in danger as well. I think it is quite a common fear for British soldiers when they do a patrol out away from the relative safety of the camps.

Potted Sun

Bright illume round in the sky,
Lifted high with rockets scream,
We watch you fly,
Showing the darkness what you mean.

As your chute opens to the breeze,
Like hands easing you gently down,
In your light everything sees,
With the colour of dark grey and soft brown.

Kass alshams called by our translator,
Sputters to life and shining bright,
Catch the prime illuminator,
Banishing the dark with your inquisitive light.

Gravity always wins your fight,
Only sixty seconds you last,
As your life dies with your life,
The darkness claims you fast.

9th October 2008

Potted Sun

*When I wrote this poem I was in Basra city attached to the infantry
(B Company, 6 Platoon), again supplying communications for
them both in the camp and on foot patrols. One night while on
stag (watch for anything suspicious and be an early warning if the
enemy is about to attack) I was thinking about being able to put
up a flare to be able to see a bit more clearly, unfortunately we
didn't have any flares where we were at the time and that started
me off again. I didn't realise until I had finished that there was
another meaning behind it.*

*It was how life was very short in the grand scheme of things
but your soul can shine and it can also be very bright in the time*

A flare (Potted Sun) being set off over Cimic House. Notice the Iraqi Army sleeping on the roof of the building to keep cool in summer. Al Qurnah. Iraq.

like a flare. This will light the features and spread to other people around you for them to see the lay of the land.

This is one such poem that I put in a few words of another language, the words "Kass alshams" are in the Arabic language and mean "Potted Sun" which is where I have taken my title. This I had to double and triple check because I had actually asked the translator how to say it and I am not exactly fluent in the language myself.

Man on Stag

There was a man on stag in Basra city,
Watching for a threat,
He didn't want anyone's pity,
For his rifle was always set.

He stood for hours on his feet,
Till they started to ache,
Because there was no comfy seat,
And sweat pooled into a lake.

Eyes are always scanning the ground,
Safety catch check the mag,
In case they come without a sound,
This is his job on stag.

He is the first defender,
The one that holds them back,
There is no faking, no pretender,
Strong will and vocal cords he can't lack.

He hopes he has good karma,
When it comes he knows what to do,
The rest don their armour,
While he screams "STAND TO!"

13th October 2008

Man on Stag on the roof of Cimic House with the Iraqi Army. There was a 30ft drop behind me when I took this picture. Al Qurnah. Iraq.

Man on Stag

This poem is about a soldiers' job when he is "On Stag" with the long hours that he could be stood there scanning the same scenery over and over again looking for any changes that might be suspicious. He is also looking for threat indicators (the abnormal in any situation such as a deserted street in a time and place that should normally be quite crowded). Stag is one of the most common jobs in the forces no matter what your corps and job and whether you are on exercises, bases and/or on operations.

Go Over There

They tell me where to go,
My feet automatically follow,
Time moves so very slow,
And my body feels so very hollow.

Off to another tour,
Another tasking,
Hundreds of miles from a store,
The mission is forever lasting.

Thinking sadly of my sisters,
When did I see them last?
While Terry clutches his daughters' pictures,
Thinking fondly of the past.

Six months we have until the end,
Six months we have already trained,
Our social lives changed to suspend,
Hoping we won't come back maimed.

Half a year feels like a whole,
Phone calls to family from afar,
It burdens the immortal soul,
With a voice that nearly says au revoir.

Our job here is finally done,
We have done our part,
To get away from this scalding sun,
Social life paused, press restart.

My body feels deeply hollow,
Time moving so very slow,
My feet automatically follow,
They tell me where to go.

19th October 2008

Go Over There

"Go Over There" is my longest poem to date being seven stanzas long. I wrote this again while I was in Basra with the Poachers (6 Platoon, B company, 2nd Battalion, The Royal Anglian Regiment). The content of the poem explains how, due to the armed forces being overstretched with its responsibility of multiple operations and how soldiers normally come from one tour only to start training for the next one, it would mean around six months to a year away.

My career is a prime example of this; when I was based in York with 2 Signal Regiment, my first year was build up training and then being on Spearhead Land Element (SLE). This was a role which involves a twenty-four hour notice to move tasking to any country, when a situation becomes too dangerous for British holiday makers and government officials to stay in that country so they have to be evacuated. This was put into reality with the conflict between Lebanon and Syria in 2006. This was literally just after we had handed over to the next troop, who went out in the end, a month after they had taken over the responsibility from us. They got called out the night that I was going to Brize Norton to fly to Qatar for a six month tour there.

Near the end of my tour there I received a phone call from the Squadron Foreman asking if I would like to go to Afghanistan when I got back for another six months. This I accepted. When I returned from the six months there, my three years at the unit had gone and it was my time to change. Germany it was.

As soon as I arrived at 7 Armoured Brigade it was straight back into training for Iraq. This, like most build up training, lasted around six months then the tour lasted for around seven months. All this, you can see, has left my social life in tatters back home and in the end it is this that the poem is about. Even if it is slightly long-winded to explain from my life − some service men and women have it even worse than that.

Medals Parade

Out for all to see,
Perfection is the key,
We march to the time,
Our boots bulled to shine.

Round and round,
Each step a snapping sound,
Seven months we've been there,
Time is ours, it's only fair.

Order in chaos,
As if it's the footie playoffs,
Back from the sands,
Memories of desolate lands.

We all stop,
We are a proud lot,
This is our medals parade,
Silver, ribbon and pin we will save.

We passed the deadly test,
Now a token on our chest,
All cheers and throw our hats,
Home at last for The Desert Rats.

26th October 2008

Getting ready to receive the Iraq Service Medal after a successful tour. Bergen, Germany. Picture by Garron Hilton.

Medals Parade

You could probably tell what I was thinking about when I wrote this poem. Home. And the last act that we do before we go on leave after our tour.

The "Medals Parade" is a celebratory parade where all soldiers that were out on tour with the Brigade and other units get their tour medal that has their number, rank and name etched on the side. I now have two medals on my chest (three including the NATO medal we get for being in Afghanistan). One being the Afghan medal and now I also have the Iraq medal. The unit that I was with was 7 Armoured Brigade based in Hohne, Germany. They have the nickname "The Desert Rats" that was given to them for fighting in the deserts in the Second World War. This will be my unit for another three years which is when I move to another one; that's if I don't get promoted first...

ROADSIDE BOMB

A roadside bomb has been found,
Hidden under unsteady ground,
Primed and ready to blast,
As soon as our boys drive past.

A cordon is placed round the site,
Just might be there till last light,
They are to stop anyone getting by;
The sentries' skin is beginning to fry.

The angry locals spit in their face,
And the interpreter is a slight saving grace,
There's only one man to get past the line,
And he's done it a hundred times.

This one man steps through the cordon,
And he was one trained in Bordon,
To the long walk he is no stranger,
On his approach to the threatening danger.

On seeing the device,
His blood turned to ice,
It's big enough to make a crater,
Thank god they didn't find it later.

It's more complex than blue, red, green,
There are more parts that aren't seen,
He tentatively removes the blasting cap,
And marks it safe on the map.

All these devices are a fatal pest,
And for now the lads can rest,
Even though they are in reduction,
There are hundreds more in production.

5th November 2008

A mock up of an American HUMVEE that had been hit by a roadside bomb. Camp Buehring, Kuwait.

Roadside Bomb

I was in the COB for two days when I thought of the start for "Roadside Bomb." I had finished most of the jobs that I needed to do at the time and I was going to get some food from the dinner hall. As I was walking to it I noticed that there were a few squaddies dressed in EOD (Explosive Ordinance Department) suits walking around the camp sweating profusely. This was in aid of "Help for Heroes Charity" and they had paid to see what it was like to do "the long walk" which is the name of the walk from the cordon to the device. The distance can vary dramatically in relation to the ground and the size of the device itself. Normally the person doing this walk will be wearing a heavy blast suit that will protect him from some of the blast if it went off as he was working on it. As you can tell it is very hard work.

On seeing these chaps doing this for charity it gave me the idea to the start of this poem. It took me a few days to finish as

63

my thoughts were often more concerned with my own job. I did not know that as the half finished poem sat in my notebook we would be called out to a roadside bomb explosion, which had hit a small American convoy in which a fellow attached radio operator was involved. As we provided the cordon on a bridge over the scene we could watch the EOD team working their way around the blast radius trying to find any evidence and forensics that they could gain concerning the maker of the device.

It was obviously coincidence that it had happened while I was in the middle of writing about the subject but it didn't stop me thinking, "Is someone having a laugh at me?" Even then I could not imagine what it would be like to clamber over a blast area being worried about another bomb on a timer waiting to finish the team off while they were rooting around or a sniper having a go, which in this case one did. Luckily he missed and did not try again.

WHITE POPPY STAINED

One by one the red petals fall,
In their place a cross stands tall,
A name carved on the front,
Reading it brings a tearful lump.

"Here lies a soldier unknown,
Who gave his life for a land of stone,
He rushed the guns on that fateful day,
And with his life he did pay."

There is a flower that we use now,
That blossoms in those fields somehow,
Even after all that discharged might,
Springs such a beautiful sight.

We remember those that fight and fought,
Who sold their lives for freedom bought,
The poppy was first white now red,
Stained with the blood of the honoured dead.

6th November 2008

White Poppy Stained

I think this poem is quite a powerful one, I wrote it on the build up to Remembrance Day. I had a thought that what if the red poppy that is used as the symbol of the end of WW1 was not red but originally white? What if it was the amount of blood that was spilt right up to the deadline was soaked up by the roots of the flower that blossomed in the fields? And, in essence, was the memory attached to that blood instilled in the flower itself?

Some of you might wonder what the "land of stone" I've put in the poem is. For me it is all the fields that are covered in crosses of the dead. These are dotted all over the world to represent people who gave their lives in the war and even though the size of the fields are huge, nearly every part of them is filled with the stone crosses.

"We remember those that fight and fought, who sold their lives for freedom bought," is a strong line; it not only touches on the past but also the present, the people that have put up their lives for the cause of their country even if they think it is wrong but because they think it is their duty to do so. They gave and give their lives so other people at home can be free to choose and be able to say it is wrong to do what they do. Such is the life of the soldier.

Believe It

If you have been there you'll know what I say,
When I talk about the Iraqi way,
For the rest it might be a surprise,
And might think it all lies.

At night it is hard to see,
Cos there's rarely any electricity,
All the cables are intermingled,
So that candles are often rekindled.

The rubbish in the streets is piled so high,
That it's impossible to pass it by,
The kids speak English all the same,
With "meester water" and "what's your name?"

The smell in the towns is so different and vile,
One sniff can make you gag for a mile,
The acidic smell of a dead carcass,
Can be used as map reference markers.

It's wise always to watch your feet,
Cos there are streams of human excrete,
When we're driving around the fact is,
That we are used for rock throwing practice.

You always hope that you won't stay long,
As you're a target for a roadside bomb,
Clutching that picture hidden in your locket,
Especially when there's an incoming rocket.

What I describe is a horrible scene,
And there are places just not foreseen,
Now you say that this can't all be true,
But I know that it's happening in Afghan too.

11th November 2008

67

MiTT OC with 6 Platoon B Company, (2nd Battalion, The Royal Anglian Regiment) out on the patrol in the streets of Basra. The Iraqi officers gave him a cup of chai (leaf tea). He described it as "quite bizarre." Notice the rubbish in the street which is typical for the city.
Basra, Iraq.

Believe It

What I really wanted for at least one of my poems is to describe Iraq so the reader does not need to imagine what it might be like. I wanted a poem that would tell them in plain English (well as much as possible in poetry). So you can see that I describe the sights, the smells and even the local kids and how they normally come up to a Westerner, throwing stones or asking for water.

I really wanted to shock the reader, who most probably has not been out to a country that has seen and experienced war on such a long timeframe.

It's not only Iraq though. Like I said in the poem, it's also Afghan that is in this state as well.

Fly Over to Holiday

I walk down the street with rifle and pack,
With sweat trickling down the small of my back,
We have been moving for many a mile,
Not always in staggered or single file.

We hide with every vehicle driving past,
Unwittingly passing us too fast,
After each one we continue in the dark,
And every house seems to bark.

As our feet tread onwards I turn my face,
And am reminded of another place,
One fondly held in my past,
And in my memory it would forever last.

This arid surrounding has seen its fill of fights,
So much that there's no power for lights,
And flying above this place of pain,
Are the flashing lights of a holiday plane.

I wonder what they see when they look down,
Do they see their countrymen covered in brown?
The dust coated faces looking back,
Wishing them a good time on their holiday pack.

19th November 2008

Flying back to civilisation from tour. Somewhere over Afghanistan.

Fly Over to Holiday

I was on my last night patrol in Iraq when I had the idea for this poem. I was second man from the front as usual because the Major liked to go first and he liked having his comms close to him. I looked up to the night sky and saw a plane clearly visible flying over us and that got me thinking, is it a civilian plane? Are there any British on that flight? And are they looking down at us while we are on patrol?

After I asked myself all these questions then I became aware that it would make a good poem and to try and make people think when they go over countries like Iraq or Afghanistan of the people that they are flying over that are not in a position to look down on anyone else and they would never be able to do it.

Then what about the other soldiers that are also in the same place, just to try and make it better and hopefully make it a place that could be respected and maybe become a major tourist and business spot for people in other countries to go to.

ALONE IN DUTY

I am here serving my time,
And I don't know where to draw the line,
I'll never see the world through your eyes,
Blissfully unaware of the living lies.

My solid presence is here,
Told how not to show any fear,
But my body is utterly hollow,
And senior commands I will blindly follow.

A womans' touch to me is xeno,
Like with you seeing a tanned albino,
My bed a cot and my duvet a sleeping bag,
Around my neck, the chain with a dog tag.

I see couples cuddle on the box,
As I numbly wash my dirty socks,
I have been told that I am like a stone,
Maybe it's why I am so alone.

What will I do when I leave?
Maybe I'll get out the gates and statue freeze,
Or maybe with my last memories be laid,
Carried by six to my last parade.

Shed no tears for my life,
For I probably won't have a wife,
I always did try to do my duty,
But some people must think I'm just loopy.

28th November 2008

Alone in Duty

I was feeling exceptionally down when I wrote this poem. I was getting ready to fly out of Iraq and to start my journey to Cyprus for decompression then back to Germany, and eventually the UK for leave. I should not have been feeling down at the time because I was at the end of another six months tour. But as I sat watching DVDs on my cot bed I watched Wall'e. *I am not normally a sentimental man but after watching this I felt very alone and home sick.*

It has been a very long time since I felt homesick, the last time that I can really remember was after I moved to my first boarding school at the age of seven years old but since then I have not really had a problem with it.

The poem itself is to portray what people have to give up so they can do their duty. When I submitted "Alone in Duty" to Forcespoetry.com, I added a little insert that I copied from a dictionary, and this is what it said:

Duty: *Noun*. The moral commitment is the sort that results in action, and it is not a matter of passive feeling or mere recognition. When someone recognizes a duty, that person commits himself/herself to the cause involved without considering the self-interested courses of actions that may have been relevant previously. This is not to suggest that living a life of duty precludes one from the best sort of life, but duty does involve some sacrifice of immediate self-interest.

I think that this explanation of the word 'Duty' is spot on and as you can see needs no more from me to describe it further. This is what I tried to describe in my poem: to do your duty well you need to put aside what other people might think to be essential to being alive.

Top Schemers

How you sit in your high-rise chair,
As if it were your own special lair,
Thinking of new random schemes,
Not really caring for what it means.

Your pen scribbles rules and plans,
Is it making it easier for them in the lands?
They work all day for your reports,
And all you say is "they are falling short."

When was the last time you were out,
Of that place where you hang about?
Is your backside moulded to the seat,
Are you allergic to the bitter heat?

Some might think you lot are sadistic,
The bodies you send home are just a statistic,
It's your plan so does it matter?
Only as long as the enemy scatter.

Your office air-con is pleasantly sweet,
But the boys outside are dead on their feet,
They fight for you with all that they own,
As you sit on your golden thrown.

7th December 2008

Top Schemers

I was very angry when I wrote this poem, at the senior staff mostly and the people that made the plans for what they thought that we should be doing. Normally they do a splendid job to the best of their abilities, but there are times when they make stupid rules that make the life of everyone a lot harder. Not only for the locals but also for the soldier that is out and doing his job on the ground while they are back in the main base, hardly ever going out of the wire.

I can't really remember why I was so angry at them but it must have been something very stupid that got in the way of me being able to do my job effectively. Making me angry does take quite a lot of work as some of my friends and family can tell you but there are just a few times when I can lose control. Most of the time I just moan and gripe more till I calm down, very occasionally I can completely lose it though. I even surprised one of my mates in the gym when we went against the boxing bags; while he was holding it I let my anger out on the bag and he had to yell at me to stop.

I'm Here Cos I'm Not All There

I'm here cos I'm not all there,
Is that why you always stare?
It's why I always have a map,
Laid out across my tender lap.

I'm here cos I'm not all there,
And it doesn't really seem fair,
The needle of my compass spins,
Trying to point to all my deadly sins.

I'm here cos I'm not all there,
And I stand halfway up or down the stair?
Where are the answers to my questions?
Can you make a few suggestions?

I'm here cos I'm not all there,
Now I'm running out of precious air,
The word is starting to go all grey,
Is this the karma that I have to repay?

I'm here cos I'm not all there,
When a hand thrusts into my musty lair,
It seems like I am an exemption,
And one loving touch will be my redemption.

11th December 2008

Pte Nicholas on the roof of Al Farahedy looking over the Shia Flats. Basra, Iraq.

I'm Here Cos I'm Not All There

"I'm Here Cos I'm Not All There" was originally a quote that I saw while I was in Iraq which I used as my signature for a while on Forcespoetry.com. After a few days I noticed that others were mentioning that they liked it and that it would be a good start for a poem. There is another poet on the site who has the handle of "Finn" and he asked if he could make a poem with the title. I agreed and told him that I will also make one and after they are both finished then we will compare the poems and see how they come out.

Around a week later I had posted my version on the site and thought it quite good, but then Finn posted his up and I have to say that I liked his version even more.

When he did post his up he said it was only half finished and still needed work even though it was at least twice as long as mine, but of course size does not matter in poetry. I am still waiting for him to finish and re-post the final version of his poem as I write this and I cannot wait till he does.

Lost in Memories

I push my way through the crowd,
For being there, I feel very proud,
The dust is blasting in my face,
And we are far from any base.

Watching for the kids' sticky fingers,
Away from my precious locket lingers,
Feeling them snag on pouch, clothing and string,
And the sun beating down on my skin.

Wherever we roam we are always on edge,
As if we were a blind man near a ledge,
Not knowing what is around the corner,
That might put our world in disorder.

I suddenly fall and hit the ground,
And wonder why there was a smashing sound,
The soaking splash of a cool liquid.
And I start to feel slightly insipid.

"OI! YOU SPILT MY DRINK!"
The translation back was so fast that I could hardly think,
Too far engrossed in my own historic fable,
That I did not see this man's table.

18th December 2008

Lost in Memories

"Lost in Memories" is about how our minds can drift into the past and relive it no matter where we are or what time it is. I placed this poem in a pub at the end but at first it is not apparent because the poem starts out as if the person is on patrol in Iraq or Afghanistan. I often think back to when I was in both countries and sometimes relive bits of it but I do not fully hallucinate like in the poem.

I was on my POTL (Post Operational Tour Leave) and had been for a week or so when I wrote this poem and of course Christmas was coming up as well so I had around six weeks leave in total. Most of the time I was down the pub having a few drinks which was where I wrote this poem.

Haunted by Haunting Eyes

I was here but now I'm gone,
And I hope that I won't be gone for long,
From the sweet embrace of your arms,
And the warm touch of your palms.

I had put my Bergen on my back,
And walked past the gate at the end of the track,
But before I went down that lane,
I looked back to the eyes of pain.

I can still see those eyes now,
They stare at me behind my eyelids somehow,
Haunting me, every time I blink,
And there's only one thing that I can think.

I see what those eyes saw that day,
A lonely figure walking away,
Out of your life once again,
To fight with brothers in foreign fen.

My eyes are hidden to hide those eyes,
With a single tear and a muffled cry,
I cannot wait to see them learn,
Of my well-being and safe return.

But even when I am back and safe,
My mind may still be in the other place,
And once again in your arms lie,
Hate again to see that haunting eye.

23rd December 2008

Haunted by Haunting Eyes

This is quite a good poem that I finished on Christmas Eve; I had started it a few days before but had trouble thinking of how it would go. When I started it I was again in the pub having a few beers when the thought of it hit me (like it often does) and I asked for a piece of scrap paper and a pen, they gave me a piece of receipt to write on.

The poem itself is about leaving a loved one to go to war and on the leaving looking back into their eyes and seeing the pain that they are going through and being haunted by the look when the soldier was leaving all the way through the tour. Even when the person that goes on tour comes back, they can still be afraid that they will most probably go back to war again.

When I go on tour I hardly think of the pain and anguish that my family goes through when I'm gone and what they must be going through. To never know who it is at the door when they hear someone knocking. I think it would be the most heart breaking experience for a family to hear that their son or daughter had been killed more than thousands of miles away and not being able to imagine how they died and my heart goes to all the families who have gone through this.

My sister was also on tour at the same time as me, and we saw each other a few times. Kandahar, Afghanistan.

81

The Hunter's Star

Every time I look at a cloudless night sky,
A group of stars always catches my eye,
Everyone knows that constellation well,
And it even shines over the gates of hell.

When I was there feeling quite alone,
I knew those stars also shone over my home,
And as I stand there admiring the view,
Wondering if you were doing it too.

But during that moment of contemplation,
There was a wild booming exclamation,
And once again we dived to the ground,
On hearing that awful, booming sound.

Explosion after explosion detonate on the camp,
Electricity goes, someone turn on his lamp,
The rockets stop, my armour's still under my desk,
I go and put it on for my post attack check,

As I depart into the desert night,
I am greeted with a dreadful sight,
Smoke billowing from a large crater,
Few wounded or time delays for later.

Now back home, every time I see those stars,
Reminds me of the places that have left scars,
Oh Hunter wherever you may shine,
Look after those brothers and sisters of mine.

5th January 2009

The Hunter's Star

"The Hunter's Star" is a poem about the star constellation of Orion and no matter where I look when I look at the stars my eyes always pick out Orion straight away, even if I am not intending to look for it. I have seen it many times when I'm in the UK, Qatar, Afghan, Iraq and Cyprus and no matter what I'm doing, I always wonder who else is looking up at those stars at the same time as I am looking at them. Is there a member of my family looking or maybe someone else that I know and love?

I remember one specific time when I was in Iraq that I was admiring the stars when the camp came under rocket attack. I had to dive to the floor for safety as we've been told to do when the alarm goes off pending an attack.

The devastation in the poem only occurred occasionally as most of the rockets either missed or were shot down by the Counter Rocket and Mortar Batteries dotted around the camp. Sometimes, however, the rockets would get through and strike the camp somewhere, although if everyone carried out the immediate action drill correctly, then the chances of being killed by a rocket was minimal unless you were unfortunate and took a direct hit.

One time one of the rockets struck the helicopter pad and damaged a few of the Apache attack helicopters, taking them out of use for quite a while, but again no one was killed.

Rise Against and Fall

The blood that is spilt in our country's name,
Is the blood of sons and families' pain,
The day their tears fell to the floor,
Was the day they closed his coffin door.

He did his job in every way,
And was proud to be serving that day,
But when that fire came round his ears,
He fought them back despite his fears.

With sweat coming out of every pore,
This is what he joined up for,
To fight the foe that wants to see,
Chaos reign in supremacy.

Through all the noise he heard a scream,
And he knew what it did mean,
He put down his arms and got into action,
With dressing applied he began the extraction.

Under fire he picked his mate up,
And that's when he ran out of luck,
The iron bolt entered his side,
And this is how he finally died.

But his extraction was a success,
And we are now only one soldier less,
He laid his life down for his mate as he,
Who died with the ultimate dignity.

As he flies home in his coffin borne,
Fulfilling the vow that he has sworn,
Now we mourn with his family's loss,
Of a soldier that will never be forgot.

22nd January 2009

Rise Against and Fall

"Rise Against and Fall" is another one of my favourite poems. It describes the last moments and actions of a soldier who, while fighting the enemy, hears one of his comrades being wounded. Even as he is still is getting shot at, the soldier puts down his only means of defending himself and first gives First Aid to the wounded comrade. He then tries to extract him so he can get more treatment by the medics and doctors.

While he is carrying his mate (which would be quite difficult on his own, as the weight of a wounded soldier with all the kit and body armour is quite heavy), he too is shot, but this time the bullet goes through his side where the body armour does not protect the person (this kind of injury is common). Though even when he gets shot he has already got his mate to the attention of the medics who saved his life but unfortunately could not do anything for the saving soldier.

The WW1 war memorial. Basra, Iraq. Picture by Garron Hilton

For me this is the ultimate sacrifice of a soldier in serving his country, family and his other soldiers in arms fighting with him. Even as he gave his life, he saved another. This is happening in Afghanistan right now, nearly every day by the people who go to extraordinary lengths to keep our freedom and for us to live without fear.

I will always think of them no matter when or where I am.

For me, Remembrance is an everyday event.

A Moment of Thought

When you go out for a drink,
What is it that you never think?
Do you ever stop half way through,
And have a moment for those that fight for you?

Do you ever raise your glass high,
For those that fight and die?
The ones that made that vow,
And for those that are fighting now.

I have my moments of contemplation,
To fill that place with no sensation,
Once a day, quiet or loud,
For the boys that make me proud.

8th February 2009

A Moment of Thought
When I wrote this poem I had been back at my unit (7 Armoured Brigade) for around a month after my post tour leave of four weeks at home with the family, friends and my girlfriend. When most soldiers come back from a tour, it is normally in their minds to relax as much as possible with them which normally involves a few (or more) drinks and late nights. I was having a few such drinks when I realised that there I was having a good time with my work mates at the end of my tour and there were lots of other soldiers still out there either starting, half way through or near the end still being tested to their limits.

This got me in one of my contemplative moods thinking about them and made a little salute in my head for them. This gave me an idea for this poem which I started to write as soon as I got back to the block.

Raindrops and Tears

The raindrops mix with my tear,
The ones I shed when I show my fears,
The scars I bear, you cannot trace,
For I always see his long dead face.

I stumble but I do not fall,
Held upright by my brothers all,
Together we stand against the strife,
To uphold freedom and for your life.

We held the book and gave the vow,
To fight and die for you right now,
I meant every word I said that day,
And to go on fighting, the glory way.

When we finally come back to you,
Please understand what we have been through,
We marched to the gates and back,
And spilt our blood on the muddy track.

All I wish to see in blossomed fruition,
Is the finish of this endless mission,
To lay content in loving faith,
And know that you are finally safe.

11th February 2009

Raindrops and Tears

Three days after writing "A Moment of Thought" I wrote this poem which is about how a soldier will give his or her life to complete the duty that he or she has vowed to do when he or she signed into the Armed Forces. Though it may cost us our minds or bodies in doing so, we would fight till the end to see our country safe.

The mindset of the people who join the Armed Forces should have the ability to shield their minds of all the things that might happen while they are in that career, more so than most of those in civilian life. Even though they may be as young as sixteen when they join (like myself) there should be potential for the growth of that mental barrier. There are those younger ones that may have gone through a cadet force of some sort before they join, maybe during or outside of school in which they may have learnt a few things.

There is also a part in this poem which describes how even though we may be scarred either mentally or physically, we always have our country, family and friends in the forces and other work colleagues that support those that have sacrificed their lives from disabling injuries. Even with these injuries they still fight on to do what they can for the country in any way that they can. This can be for different reasons, but I think the main one is because they still feel the fire of duty in their hearts and the people around them support them in the only way that they can because it is the bond of the brotherhood and family that gets them through it.

THROUGH THE VALLEY

As I walk through the valley of blood and sweat,
My rifle is cocked and my mind is set,
Brother to my left and to my right,
If anything happens we are prepared to fight.

It feels like I have been here all my life,
Going against those who would do us strife,
My body has changed with my mind,
When you look at me what do you find?

Maybe a gung-ho soldier who can't let go,
And no matter where, he sees his foe,
Maybe you see a man lonely in desperation,
Who lives in cold desolation.

Well, I plan to fight no matter the cost,
Like all those before me whom we have lost,
And if they put my dog tags in your palm,
You know I went to protect you from harm.

17th February 2009

On the Tacsat during the simulated supply drop in Bavaria. Germany.

Through The Valley

In "Through The Valley" I describe a little of the change that a mind goes through when it has been subverted by a force of pressure for a long time like the different mindset of a soldier. Where some may look at a problem as a difficulty, we see it as a challenge. Even though when we are given an order from a more senior rank that simply baffles us in every way and aspect, we still get the job done (there may be a lot of "quiet" comments of how it should be done or even not done at all with ten really good and real reasons why it would be a bad idea).

I Am But...

I am but a grain of sand,
Pretending to be part of this land,
Sifting through the plains of strife,
Trying to figure what to do with this life.

I am the grass that plays in the wind,
Swaying in the breeze on those that sinned,
Happy in the rays of brilliant light,
Being crushed by a hate filled blight.

I am but a flake of snow,
White in the drift, watch me flow,
Stained red with blossomed poppy I be,
Frozen forever but still wonderfully free.

7th March 2009

I Am But...

"I Am But..." is one of the only spiritual poems that I have written. I was in my room in Hohne when I wrote this and I was feeling a little bit uncertain about who I was. I think that many people have these thoughts in their life. Have I made the right decisions? Is this who I am meant to be? Could I have done better?

I thought long and hard about what I do for a living and realised that for me I had made the right choices and I am proud of it. I would absolutely hate to be behind a desk doing the same thing over and over again. In the Army every day is different, mainly because something comes in the middle of what you were doing so it makes it take ten times as long and three times harder but that's a part of the challenge. Although I bet that if I stay in the army for so long then I probably will end up behind a desk, but even then there will be some things that will keep me on my feet. It might be a good time to think about moving on by then though.

The Weight of Forever

My bones creak with the weight of forever,
Around my neck is tied a leaded tether,
I remember the places I have been,
Especially most of the horrors I have seen.

I never forget the smell of death,
How its acrid stench burns your breath,
The sight of its eyeless gaze,
Forever in my mind it plays.

An uncontrolled memory,
In a chaotic symphony,
The sweat rolls down my back,
I'm having another panic attack.

The fog of war clouds my eyes,
My pulse begins to rise,
I thought my test was done,
And this for me it did stun.

I hope this will soon end,
And that I could talk with a friend,
Someone who also knows this test,
To combat combat stress.

14th March 2009

The Weight of Forever

I have been a member of a website called Forcespoetry.com for quite a while now. They are trying to become a charity to help with and spread the awareness of PTSD (Post Traumatic Stress Disorder) which is more commonly known as combat stress or Gulf War Syndrome.

The website aims to help those that have it through poetry, either getting them to write or read poems from those that also suffer from it. PTSD normally strikes those that have been affected by an extremely traumatic event such as rape, kidnap, combat, road accidents or even a medical operation. Many of the sufferers can feel depressed, anxious, grief stricken and angry. With these there can also be other symptoms that attribute itself to PTSD such as flashbacks/nightmares, avoidance and being on guard nearly all the time. Due to all these symptoms the sufferer can also experience muscle aches and pains, diarrhoea, headaches, irregular heartbeats, feelings of panic or fear, depression, heavy drinking and drug abuse (mostly painkillers). As you can imagine this can cause quite a bit of distress for all involved including family, friends and loved ones.

No one yet knows what causes PTSD but quite often people believe that having it is a sign of weakness. It is not as it can happen to absolutely anyone after such an event. People may think that it is their fault if someone close is suffering from it because the sufferer may get sudden mood swings or become panicked at sudden noises such as doors closing suddenly or someone starting to talk behind them when they thought no one was there.

The best way to get better if you find that you do have it is to talk to someone. It might be someone that has also been where the event took place; even writing it down can help. It has been known for those that suffer to write in to the website and thank them for their help; even though they did not realise it. Just getting it out there for people to see can save lives if someone has become suicidal.

This is what I try to get through with my poem in simple words so anyone can understand and hopefully get as much help as is needed for it.

TERMINUS EST

My mind is dry and my words are gone,
Never again to play that beautiful song,
I feel sometimes hollow and numb,
And the old stuff is no longer fun.

I have travelled to places so far away,
The places whose description you can't say,
The desert stretches off to a distant hill,
Where the enemy waits for our boys to kill.

But it's not just in those hills we fight,
Also in the river banks green we bite,
Our teeth as sharp as the executioner's sword,
Again and again we take on the horde.

Every time we do, more British blood is spilt,
And every time we wade back through the silt,
We ask why we always give it back,
The brass just says "it's cos the troops we lack."

So again and again we go out to claim,
The source of so much blood and pain,
No matter what, I fight with the best,
But the wind there whispers "Vobis Terminus Est."

31st March 2009

Terminus Est

"Terminus Est" is a poem about a town in Helmand Province on the river Helmand in Afghanistan called Sangin when I was on tour in Kandahar Province. While I was doing my job it felt as if nearly every week an operation will go out and take Sangin from the Taliban. I am not sure if it was like this but it did seem like it.

We would mount an offensive to take it, most of the Taliban heard us coming and ran away leaving mines and IEDs (Improvised Explosive Devices) for our troops to stumble into. Some of them also stay behind and take them on with small arms and RPGs (Rocket Propelled Grenades). This is where we would lose a few of our troops each time they went out to secure Sangin.

Due to the lack of manpower in Afghanistan most of the time we would have to pull back to the nearest forward operating base and leave Sangin for the Taliban to re-take. This would happen over and over again and it was not only here that this to-ing and fro-ing would occur. In the fourth stanza the soldiers ask why we always fall back after we have secured it at the cost of soldiers' lives and the seniors would reply that they would order it if only they had enough men to keep a force big enough to keep it secure.

The title of the poem can be translated from "Terminus Est" to become "this is the end." At the finish of the poem the wind whispers over the fjord "Vobis Terminus Est".

This means "For you this is the end."

Me posing besides a SNATCH landrover just before we deployed into Kandahar City with the Pioneers. Kandahar Airfield, Afghanistan.

In Virum Perfectum

There is a great king on a hill,
I left his halls naught half a century and one past,
And I ride the fate of time still,
Thinking that he will forever last.

After a long battle with the beast, I had to rest,
And the kind king bade me a bed to stay,
And as I wandered his cloisters once more,
The same hall unchanged that I used to pray.

Only the tapestries have changed,
Not the walls, not the floors, not the masters,
Just more wrinkles and manes but the same smiles,
Smiles that are tired of the ouroboros of time.

There used to be rooms full of learning and studies,
Now empty and barred to those that dare,
Only half the scholars remain now,
Not seeing the empty spaces in the next chair.

The brave warriors that trained each week,
Used to fill the parade square to full,
Now hardly a platoon of unwilling,
Still heckled by the Frosty drill master.

I remember the king's court being the envy of the realm,
Now old and decrepit coats,
It lasted a hundred years before my time,
But the crumbling walls have finally given to its ghosts.

I turn away with a heavy and troubled soul,
The mirror of my departure before,
For it pains me to leave this king close to death,
But the trumpets call me back to war.

So adieu kind king on the hill,
Remember me as I remember you,
A bright academy sparkling and gay,
In your annals I will forever stay, adieu.

I shall weep forever for your past glory,
In virum perfectum.

3rd April 2009

In Virum Perfectum

Whilst on Easter leave I visited my old school near Chipping Norton in Oxfordshire. I had left around six years before to start my career as a soldier in the British Army after completing my GCSEs. The name of the school was Kingham Hill School, hence the king on the hill in the poem as it gives it an almost rustic quality and it does not fully connect with the school itself.

The title "In Virum Perfectum" is the motto for the school which translates as, "Unto a Perfect (or complete) man." These words are from Ephesians 4 v.13, and in a more modern translation are rendered as "to mature manhood". This also connects to the school in another hidden way.

Before I arrived back at the school for my visit I was expecting a lot to have changed over time but when I got there I discovered that nearly everything was exactly the same apart from the posters on the walls in which I describe as "tapestries" to fit into the poem.

Also in the poem I describe the teachers being stuck in the "ouroboros of time". This is kind of a time loop. Ouroboros is from the Greek which means "tail-devouring snake" and the symbol of it is exactly that depicting a serpent or a dragon eating its own tail which never ends because it also re-creates itself. It is also commonly known in other cultures through the phoenix that burns itself then rises again from the ashes. The teachers are much like this; with each term that goes past they have to start all over again with new pupils, only gaining more wrinkles and less hair.

What I also noticed while I was visiting was that most of the classrooms that where normally full while I was learning there were mostly empty on my visit and the place seemed quite empty especially between classes with pupils going to their next lessons. When I was a student at Kingham I was in the CCF (Combined Cadet Force) which was one of the extracurricular activities there which had the numbers of a good hundred when fully paraded in front of the school's main building. But when I revisited there was only around a platoon's worth on the parade which is at a number of thirty people.

There is also a mention of "the Frosty drill master" who was the RSM (Regimental Sergeant Major) called Mr Frost who is an ex-tanky who was really the first man who had a bit of military bearing that demanded everyone's respect as he had been there and done it all as a real live soldier.

Names On The Wall

I walk past each grave in turn,
Looking at each name,
A man stands before one, the same in its tier,
A tear runs down his cheek,
Salutes the stone with his best,
I see him every year.

I look out to where the names are left,
New names are there those that fight today,
I leave these men to their rest.
How many more have to pay?

My shoulders begin to sag,
But raise again by a flutter,
I look up at the crossed red, white, and blue flag,
And under my breath for them a prayer that I mutter.

I look back at the names on the wall,
So many red with blood and pain,
I read each one in turn and where they did fall,
Until with a shock I see my own chiselled name.

8th April 2009

The WW1 war memorial. Basra, Iraq. Picture by Garron Hilton.

Names On The Wall

This poem took a while to produce, after the first time I wrote it stayed in my notebook for months taking a long time before I was truly happy with the finished product. It is about being in a war cemetery looking at the graves and reading the names of those that have fallen.

On looking up, the character sees another man looking at a certain grave and crying as if weeping for a fallen comrade that fell in a long ago war when he did not and remembering the brotherhood that was felt between them.

In my mind I imagine it being quite misty around and having a slight chill from the wind that is flapping the union flag around on the flag post. There is a slight twist in at the end where the character looks at the "Names On The Wall" again and gets a very nasty shock when he sees his own name chiselled in.

GLORY ROAD

The flames have scorched the sky to dusk,
The black snowflakes fall with but a whisper,
The whistle of torn air with the beat of the drum,
The forever war goes on unknown.

My boot prints are gold in my toiling passage,
The wasteland of this once pure city stretches on,
Forever at the turning of the clock,
We march on down glory road.

At times I pass the echoes of those before,
And those of battles that are yet to be,
With the standards and marching flutes,
File after file of the dead salute.

Never stopping after the first fight was written,
The list of those lost stretches forever,
Is there enough ink in the world,
For all those that walk down glory road?

8th April 2009

Glory Road

"Glory Road" is a poem that I wrote about the road to hell and what you might see while marching down it to the gates. The ground being black from the dust of the burnt cities and towns that litter the way and each step reveals the golden sand underneath that had been turned over in the footprints. There are also the ghosts that you would pass on the way from the wars that have been fought in the past and the future deaths of wars to come.

If you think about it, Britain has rarely gone without a conflict during the history of our country. Only in a few times has there been peace in which none of its soldiers are going out to fight the enemy of the time and I believe that it may carry on like that for a very long time indeed.

Can we continue like this? If we do become a peaceful country then I think we would lose a part of ourselves eventually and maybe turn against each other.

Every Day I Kill

I killed a man today,
It happened in my waking,
I looked in the mirror and there he was,
His heart forever breaking.

I killed a child today,
He was in my head playing,
And in three ranks at attention standing,
Into the past he fades praying.

I killed my love today,
It was in my heart singing,
But in my rifles report it fled,
And in its place it leaves a stinging.

I killed a soldier this afternoon,
It was when I took off those clothes,
And when I sit and talk with my friends,
The ghosts of the child and man in me flows.

13th May 2009

Every Day I Kill

I wrote this poem when I was back at my unit a full month and a bit after my last poem was written. With the big time gap between poems I was starting to think that I might be losing the knack to write poems but, after getting into the right state of mind, I thought about things to inspire me again.

This poem is about how soldiers can change when they put on and take off their uniforms. As soon as the uniform goes on in the morning then there is a transformation that hides all those things that make the person identifiable to his friends and family; this is to make himself a better soldier and when he is out on tour wherever it may be, then the last thing that he might think about is what someone is doing twenty thousand miles away when he should really be wondering where the next shot or bomb might go off.

When he comes back though and puts his civilian clothes back on then all the old feelings and the things that make him who he is start to come back to him.

This poem is also in another anthology from Forcespoetry.com called Voices of the Poppies. After a voting competition during 2009, "Every Day I Kill" was voted as one of my best poems.

My Wandering Muse

My muse has gone a'wandering,
Far away from my head,
It's been so long I wonder,
If he has fallen in the gutter dead.

My hand has ceased its scribbling,
Before it has begun,
And the pages stay blank before me,
Like a shadow from the dusk sun.

But maybe it is not all gone,
Maybe it is only sleeping,
For the occasional twitch in my dreams,
With the sheep over the fence leaping.

I am now only half of the old me,
Trying to recreate that symphony,
With scattered notes all over,
Trying to grasp the puzzle's litany.

There will be a time when it returns,
And guides my gentle quill,
I will feed it with all that is me,
Until again it has had its fill.

25th May 2009

*On the open firing range just outside the security fences of the COB.
With 4Platoon, B Company, 2nd Battalion, The Royal Anglian Regiment.
Basra, Iraq*

My Wandering Muse

*When I wrote this poem I again thought that my ability to write
poetry had dried up after all this time; the first poem that I wrote
whilst I was in Afghanistan and the few that I wrote after this
one were just a coping mechanism. Poetry is something to keep my
brain ticking to deal with all the stress of being out on tour and
being on edge all of the time, just in case the enemy might attack
with rockets on the camp (which happened frequently). Especially
in Afghanistan while I was in Kandahar and it happens without
warning unlike being on the COB in Iraq where the early
warning alarm would sound before the rockets hit the ground and
the phalanx guns would try to shoot the rounds out of the sky
before they did any damage.*

*Being home for so long dulled my sense of inspiration; it is as
if my poetry mind is not as sharp as it once was while I was out*

there. Maybe it is the thought and feeling that something might happen at any time and you have to react to it spontaneously, which is what we are trained to do. What happens though when we return from being through that for such a time?

Even my dad or any other person who has been in that situation can tell you that when you return you are still on edge for a while afterwards, every fibre in your body is poised to jump in the nearest bush or under a table with every loud noise.

This can be quite problematic if you've just come off tour and it is Guy Fawkes Day with lots of fireworks flying around.

FIGHT FOR NAUGHT

When we return back from war,
It is hard to see what we are fighting for,
All that violence on the sand,
Is mimicked like a mime in this land.

All the blood leaked from our veins,
With all the loss and the bitter pains,
It seems like it comes to naught,
Just a motion in the way we fought.

We see the rot in our society,
While you believe you are a deity,
And all the pleasures that you inhale,
Buys the enemy the guns for sale.

If only you could stand away and see the change,
Your breast will also fill with rage,
A few are good I will admit,
But most really makes me sick.

25th July 2009

Fight For Naught
As you can probably tell from the tone, this is quite an angry poem. Although the support of the public in the last couple of years has grown magnificently and I feel pride whenever I am given a hand shake or even a free beer (which has happened a few times). Whilst living out in Germany and on tour I have noticed the change and differences in the United Kingdom. Even though the support is a lot better, the amount of crime seems to be a lot worse in most ways. In taking a step back you get to notice a lot more than you normally world.

When we go to Afghanistan or have briefings on drugs we are always told, "Over 90% of the heroin on the UK's streets originates from Afghanistan" and, "The drugs and the insurgents are linked". This gets me very angry whenever I think that a British citizen taking drugs for pleasure can spend thousands of pounds on their addiction. With the money that has eventually found its way down the chain back to Afghan an insurgent can buy even more weaponry, rounds, explosives, rockets and many more to use against our troops that are out there. You can really say that part of the UK funds the enemy. Although there are a few reasons why we buy opium from a few farmers to supply for medical supplies such as morphine.

Nijmegen Death March

Going down the town,
And over the seven hills,
The long way round,
With a body full of pills.

All of my blisters have burst,
The feelings drained from my limbs,
This really is the worst,
So where is my promised Pimms?

With the screaming of the crowd,
And the marching boots of an army,
It is something to make you proud,
So why do it? because it is so barmy.

We are going for our medal,
For this new sensation,
I am shaking hands with the devil,
On the four day march in Nijmegen.

23rd July 2009

Nijmegen Death March

I have to say that this is the single most painful thing I have so far ever done. The Nijmegen Marches are both for military and civilians. Of course I did the military side of the march which was to walk at speed carrying ten kilograms of weight (without water), around fifteen kilograms (with water) for one hundred miles. This is done over four days so in total we had to march twenty-five miles per day. Most people would shrug and say "That's easy!" but to say the least, on day one I developed eight blisters on my feet and had to be seen to by medical staff to be popped, padded and strapped. On the third day I was in absolute agony and it felt like I was walking on rusted nails. It was on this day when

The entire team (207 Sig Sqn and 208 (Liverpool) Field Hospital (V) with the individual medals on their chests and the shield for "The Best Land Team", Nijmegen.

we were walking over the Seven Hills as mentioned in the poem, that it started to rain. With morale low, wet and in pain I was asked by my sergeant to compose a poem by the second rest stop, so while we marched I wrote.

When we got to the rest stop it was still raining and one of the newer privates had forgotten his gortex jacket so was being berated about it. It was while this was happening that I asked if I should read my poem out. It certainly calmed him down and while I read it out there where a few bits of laughter and giggles from the inside jokes in the poem.

On the fourth and final day of the march quite a few of us where a lot better, mainly because we had found out how well Paracetamol and Ibuprofen worked.

When we finally crossed the finish line we were given our individual medals and the shield for "The Best Land Team".

I don't know how they figured this one out, maybe because we were always waving at the crowds in every town that we entered or heckling other teams whenever we passed them no matter the amount of pain we were in at the time.

What they didn't realise (even though it was the top brass's idea) was that we were actually two separate units made into one team of twenty, and when they gave out the shield they found out that we were the first team to ever win this prize as an amalgamation of two teams. Half of the team came from my unit in Hohne (207 Signals Squadron) and the other half was from a Territorial Army unit in Liverpool (208 Field Hospital (V)).

I was on a personal mission on this march as well because when I told my Mother about it she said that my Father had done it when he was seventeen, so I had to do it not just for personal pride but also the family pride as well. I didn't tell anyone on the team about this until right at the end. I also have a name tag on my uniform that was my Dad's when he was a serving member, and I wore that on the last two days of the march. Whenever I felt particularly bad I would always think of the name on that name tag that I was wearing. I even take it on tour with me as well.

THE SOLDIER POETS

Wherever there is a war,
A poet will surely be there,
With a rifle in his hands,
And bullets rushing through his hair.

Like all of his brothers,
He will stand and fight,
Till his very last breath,
Under the sun's blistering light.

His every feeling and thought,
Will be written by his bloodied hand,
Not asking for your forgiveness,
But for you to understand.

If I was to die in any way,
I would hope not to be alone,
But with those brothers on the front,
And maybe have a poem on my headstone.

4th August 2009

The Soldier Poets

This poem is about how in every single conflict that the world has seen there has been at least one poet right there in the centre of it doing his job as a soldier. No matter what the overall mission was there was always someone there who would write down their insights of what they had seen, heard or felt at the time in which their mind is on, although many might not get their thoughts out into the open because of a lot of different reasons.

Being one of the few poets that serve my country I feel privileged to get the message out of what it is like to be a soldier. Joining the forces got me to find my muse in poetry as well, I only started to write when I was on tour in Afghanistan and that was the beginning of my writing on my life. No doubt that when I do die then I will have a poem on my headstone so even in death the message can still be read by the people that walk past and read the stone. The greatest honour I believe in my passing would be on the front line.

I wrote this poem while I was on summer leave after Nijmegen, letting my feet recover. I was back in Flan O'Briens in Bath again when I wrote this poem (I do not know why but it stirs the muse in me) and as soon as I finished I asked one of the punters next to me what they thought about it. It was then that I found out that there was an open mic night at the Royal Oak pub that very night. So that night, that was where I could be found.

I was on around fourth after a few of the other acts and I would be the first poet to read that night as the ones before where musicians and singers. When my name was called I was extremely nervous and I was actually shaking but I still read on. While I listened to the other acts before mine I found out that some people continued to talk quite vocally with each other in the corner and I hoped that they would not with mine.

I started with what I did and where I'd been, and as soon as the pub heard that I was in the Army and that I'd been on a few tours the whole room went silent. This really surprised me and

The sun sets over Camp BASTION in Helmand Province, Afghanistan.

made me even more nervous than before. I read out four of my poems and at the end there was a huge round of applause and a lot of handshakes as well. Afterwards quite a few people came up to me to talk about the Army, about the support that they get, about the war and about everything military that they could think of. One lass also said that she nearly cried listening to my poetry which really did shock me quite a lot. The barman was also kind enough to give me a few free drinks, though he didn't tell me the reason for it. They went down very nicely though!

I believe that in the limbo between tours the writing of poetry will trickle out of me until we start the build up training again to go back out for another six months and then it again will flow as never before. One can only hope. I write whatever my mind puts together for itself, I may be doing something completely different when my mind just clicks and comes out with a sentence that will normally be the start (or middle) of a poem. I have found that at certain times it becomes easier for me to start to write a poem or two; this is in the dead of the night when I am quite tired and my mind starts to wander. Even when I am alert a poem will normally just pop into my head. You might think that I would keep awake for so long every night to see what comes to me, but that's not a normal thing for me to do.

Most of these poems were written when I was on tour either in Afghanistan or Iraq. I do not know why but war brings out the poet in a few people. Whilst I was in Iraq I found out that there was another poet out on the same tour who was writing his works at the same time as me. When he went on BFBS (British Forces Broadcasting Service) most of my colleagues thought it was me even though I was in the Shia Flats miles away from the base at the time. His name is B.J. Lewis. He's from Newcastle and he works in the RAF.

While he was out in Iraq, B.J. was also working in the C-RAM (Counter Rocket and Mortar batteries), mainly consisting of heavy duty automated Mini-guns that shoot any incoming rockets or mortars (hence the name) out of the sky before they can land and do any damage to anyone or anything on the base. After I found that B.J. was working on this, every time I was on camp and heard the thunder of these awesome weapons firing I silently thanked him for doing such a brilliant job for keeping them up and running.

Later I found out that B.J. was also a member of Forcespoetry. com and we swapped a few words together. I'm sure that many more poets will appear whilst out on tour and I hope that I'll be able to meet a few of them and discuss our work in both the poetic and military sense. And maybe have a few pints in the process.

Six Months Later

by B.J. Lewis

It feels a lifetime ago since I was there.
But I can still taste the atmosphere, feel the warm air.
We've bid farewell to that war now, we've counted our
dead,
We've dusted ourselves down and refocused ahead.

But there's no rest for old soldiers, there's still work to do,
British lives still expire in conflict anew,
As I learn of the bloodshed from the comfort of home
I relive those old feelings and let my thoughts roam.

For although I remember the hardship endured,
There's a voice deep within me that can't be ignored,
It compels my return to the adventure of war,
It wants to feel more alive, like it did do before.

Me in the sangar on the roof (lookout) on Cimic house. Al Qurnah, Iraq.

MY LIFE TIMETABLE

1986   Birth, 21st November.

1993   Student at Swanbourne House School,
Buckinghamshire.

2000   Student at Kingham Hill School, Oxfordshire.

2003   Signed up to the Army at age 16.
Basic Training at Arbourfield Army Technical
Foundation College.

2004   Finished trade training at Blandford, Dorset.

2005   Posted to 2 Signal Regiment,
214 Signal Squadron, Yorkshire.

2006   Put on Spearhead Land Element (SLE) for 6 months,
twenty-four hours notice to move to any
country that needs assistance. Tour to Qatar.

2007   Tour to Afghanistan.

2008   Posted to 7 Armoured Brigade (The Desert Rats),
207 Signal Squadron. Tour to Iraq.

2009   Nijmegen 100 (2009) Marches.
Promoted to Lance Corporal.